MOLECULES and ATOMS

Troll Associates

MOLECULES and ATOMS

by Rae Bains

Illustrated by Chuck Harriton

Troll Associates

Library of Congress Cataloging in Publication Data
Bains, Rae.
 Molecules and atoms.

 Summary: Explains how all matter is composed of atoms,
which join together to form molecules, and how scientists
have learned to release energy by splitting the atom.
 1. Atoms—Juvenile literature. 2. Molecules—
Juvenile literature. [1. Atoms. 2. Molecules]
I. Harriton, Chuck, ill. II. Title.
QC173.16.B35 1985 539.7 84-2712
ISBN 0-8167-0284-5 (lib. bdg.)
ISBN 0-8167-0285-3 (pbk.)

Copyright © 1985 by Troll Associates, Mahwah, New Jersey
All rights reserved. No part of this book may be used
or reproduced in any manner whatsoever without written
permission from the publisher.
Printed in the United States of America
10 9 8 7 6 5 4 3 2 1

Everything in the world that has weight and fills space is called matter. Your body is made up of matter. A school desk is matter. So is the air we breathe, the water in the ocean, the leaves on a tree, and snowflakes.

Matter can be in the form of a solid, such as a rock. It can be in the form of a liquid, such as milk. Or it can be in the form of a gas, such as the helium used to fill balloons.

All matter—solid, liquid, or gas—is made up of very small particles called atoms. There are billions and billions of atoms in one drop of water or in a single grain of sugar. Atoms are so small that they can be observed only through the most powerful electron microscopes.

Atoms join together to form molecules of different kinds of matter. A molecule of water contains 2 hydrogen atoms and 1 oxygen atom. A molecule of sugar contains 12 carbon atoms, 22 hydrogen atoms, and 11 oxygen atoms. The exhaust fumes given off by a car's engine contain carbon monoxide, which is a gas. A molecule of carbon monoxide contains 1 carbon atom and 1 oxygen atom.

A molecule is a basic unit of matter. It is the smallest unit that has all the building blocks that make up any kind of matter. For example, if any one of the atoms of hydrogen or oxygen that make up a molecule of water is removed, the matter is no longer water. For water to exist, there must be molecules with 2 parts hydrogen to 1 part oxygen. In the same way, if any one of the carbon, hydrogen, or oxygen atoms is removed from a sugar molecule, the matter is no longer sugar.

There are more than 100 kinds of atoms. They are known as elements. Most of the elements in the world exist in nature. A few of the elements, however, have been created by scientists working in laboratories. Some of the elements can be seen in a pure form. For instance, gold, silver, lead, and mercury are pure elements.

Most of the time, however, elements are not found by themselves. Most elements that make up matter are combined with other elements. When this happens, the molecules they create are called chemical compounds. Water is the chemical compound made up of the elements hydrogen and oxygen.

The atoms of each element are different from the atoms of every other element. The difference is the number of particles that make up the atom. Every atom consists of particles called protons, neutrons, and electrons. The protons and neutrons form the core of the atom and are called the nucleus. The electrons form the shell of the atom.

The nucleus of an atom might be compared to the sun at the center of our solar system. The electrons might be compared to the planets that travel around our sun. Between the electrons and the nucleus, there is a great deal of space. In fact, most of an atom is space.

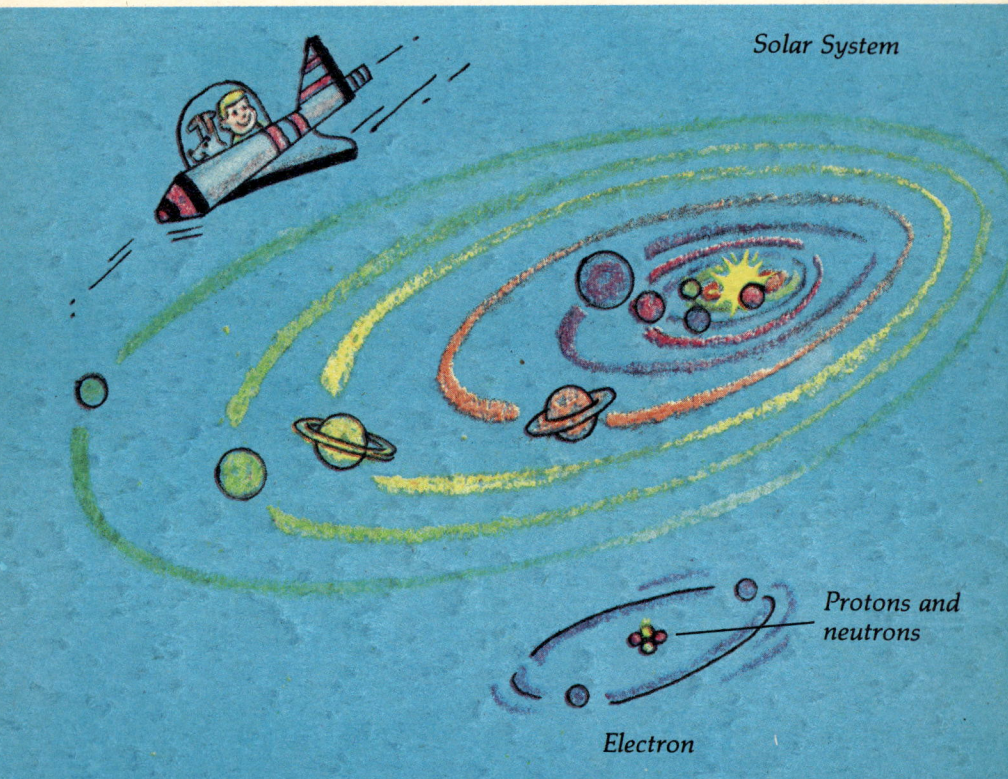

Solar System

Protons and neutrons

Electron

Imagine that the nucleus of an atom is the size of a pencil eraser. In that case, the electrons would be the size of bits of dust and would be a quarter of a mile from the eraser. The whole atom would then measure about a half-mile across. And most of that half-mile would be empty space.

The protons in an atom's nucleus have a positive electrical charge. The neutrons in the atom's nucleus are the same size and weight as protons, but they have no electrical charge. *Neutron*, in this sense, stands for "neutral."

The electrons that travel around the nucleus of an atom have a negative electrical charge. Every atom has the same number of electrons and protons. The electrical attraction between the protons in the atom's nucleus and the atom's orbiting electrons keeps the atom from flying apart.

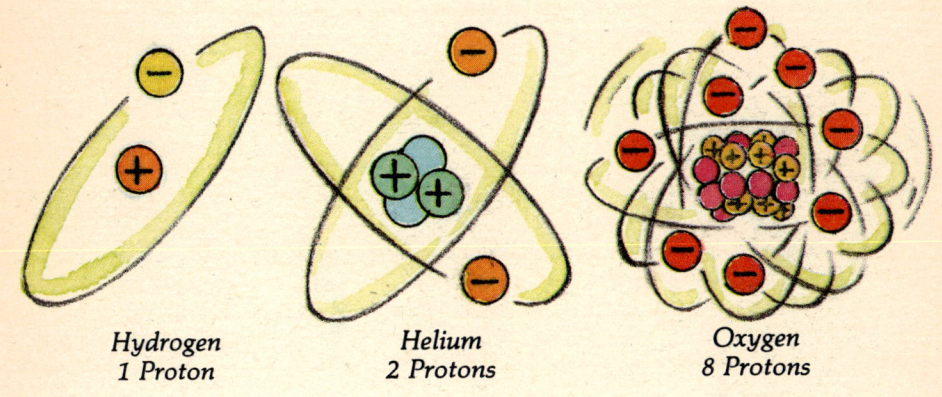

Hydrogen
1 Proton

Helium
2 Protons

Oxygen
8 Protons

Elements are classified according to a system of atomic numbers. For example, the element called hydrogen has 1 proton, so hydrogen is given the atomic number 1 on the list of elements. The element called helium has 2 protons in each atom, so its atomic number is 2. Oxygen has 8 protons, so its atomic number is 8. The number of neutrons in an atom is not considered in deciding an element's atomic number.

An atom's weight is equal to the total number of its protons and neutrons. The atom called carbon-12 has 6 protons and 6 neutrons, so it has an atomic weight of 12, or 12 atomic mass units. Uranium has 92 protons and 146 neutrons, so its atomic weight is 238, which is the sum of 92 and 146.

The electrons in an atom, although they are equal to the number of protons, are not figured into an atom's atomic weight. That is because they are so light that they have almost no weight at all. The electrons of any atom are almost 2,000 times lighter than the protons of the same atom.

Most of the knowledge scientists have about atoms has been discovered within the last century. But the idea that matter was composed of particles too small to see goes back to ancient times.

Long ago, Greek philosophers were the first people to suggest that the smallest part of matter would be something that could not be cut into anything smaller. In fact, that is what the word *atom* means.

Today, we know that atoms are not the smallest particles, since they are composed of still smaller particles—protons, electrons, and neutrons. Other particles include mesons, neutrinos, and hyperons. There are about 100 identified kinds of subatomic particles. And there are probably other subatomic particles yet to be discovered.

The subatomic particles known today differ from the three basic particles—electrons, protons, and neutrons. Most of these subatomic particles come into existence only when atoms are broken apart in laboratory experiments. And they generally do not remain in existence for more than a very brief time.

We cannot see the atoms that make up matter, but we can see matter itself. That is because atoms stick together to form molecules. And when there are enough molecules sticking together, we are able to see the matter they form.

For example, we cannot see a molecule of water. But we can see a drop of water, which is made up of billions of molecules. And each of these molecules contains 2 hydrogen atoms to 1 oxygen atom. This is true whether the water molecule is in the form of a gas, a liquid, or a solid. It remains water so long as the atoms in the molecule stay together.

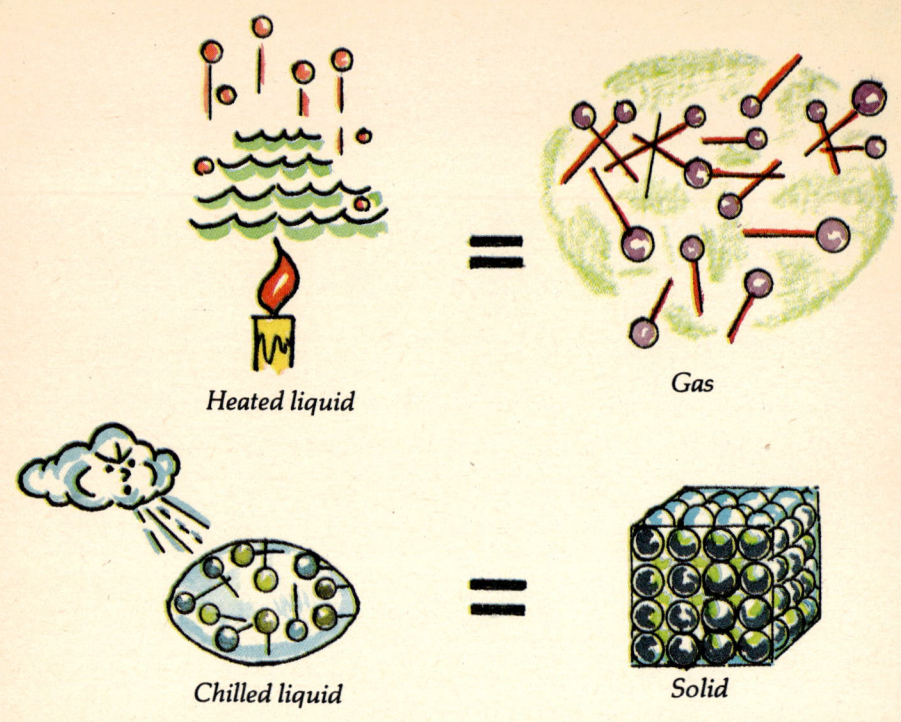

Water and most other elements can be changed from a gas to a liquid, or from a liquid to a solid by heating or cooling. When we boil liquid water, it evaporates, or turns to gas. When we freeze liquid water, it turns to a solid called ice. The molecules have not changed in structure, but their attraction for each other has changed.

All molecules are constantly in motion. When they are heated, the motion grows faster. This speed begins to weaken the attraction the molecules have for each other. So, when you boil water, the molecules fly apart from each other to form a gas.

Cooling has the opposite effect on molecules. When molecules get colder, their motion grows slower. Now they begin to place a greater attraction on each other. When water is frozen, the molecules move slowly and join together to form the solid matter we call ice.

Scientists say that every form of matter can be changed from gas to liquid to solid, and back again, if the conditions are right. But the amount of cold needed to freeze some elements—like helium and hydrogen, for example—does not naturally exist on Earth. Nor is it possible, under normal Earth conditions, to turn lead into gas.

Most of the atoms that make up matter in our everyday world are said to be stable. That is, they do not give off radiation. This is true whether the matter is composed of single elements, such as iron, or a combination of elements, such as water.

However, there are elements in nature, such as uranium and radium, that are radioactive. That is, they give off radiation. These elements have unstable atoms. Radioactive elements have complicated cores, or nuclei. These nuclei break down, giving off

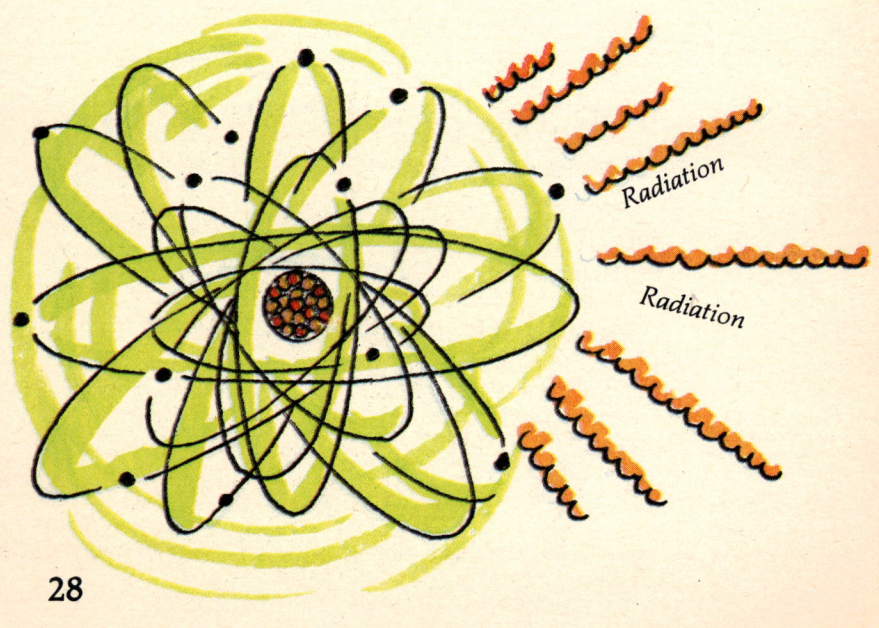
Radiation
Radiation

radiation until the atoms are changed into a more stable form. Only then does the radiation stop.

Once scientists learned that splitting an atom's nucleus causes the atom to give off radiation, the world had entered the atomic age. Smashing the atom in a machine known as a cyclotron resulted in the discharge of a huge amount of radiant energy.

This process of splitting atoms—called nuclear fission—has been used to create highly destructive wartime weapons, as well as to produce electrical power for homes and industry, for medical research and treatment, and for research into the nature of our world.

Someday, scientists hope to be able to produce energy by atomic fusion. Fusion, which is the joining together of atoms, is the process by which the sun produces the enormous amounts of energy that heat and light the solar system. And scientists also hope that, someday, nuclear energy will safely supply the answers to many of the world's biggest problems.